In this Interactive Workbook & Journal

BRAVE VISION

YOU HAVE TO SEE IT | TO BUILD IT

CONTENTS

THE "I" CHART
UNDERSTANDING WHERE VISION STARTS & HOW IT ENDS

THE APPOINTMENT
THE HISTORY & SYMPTOMS SHEET

THE "I" EXAM VERSUS THE "EYE" EXAM
A SERIES OF TESTS THAT MEASURE A PERSON'S OCULAR & INTERNAL HEALTH AND VISUAL STATUS FOR THE ABILITY TO SEE

THE COVER TEST & FOCUS ANALYSIS
IDENTITY DISSECTION TO DETERMINE YOUR PERCEPTION

THE BUILDING TOOLS
THE SHOVEL | THE SEEDS | THE TRASH BAG

THE DAMASCUS REFRACTION
RECEIVING YOUR PRESCRIPTION TO SEE

THE DISCRETIONARY IMPARTATION
THE TIMING OF THE OCULAR & INTERNAL RELEASE

BRAVE VISION
THE SEER & THE BUILDER

Brave Vision -
The second in the Be Brave Series
builds the foundation on why Vision has nothing to do you what you see out of your eyes but what you
perceive to see through your heart and mind. Khalilah, once again drives you to a place that breaks the stereotype of what many
may say to tell you what you need to hear.

Brave Vision is the act or power of sensing with the eyes but
includes a wider range of visual abilities and other sensory skills.
It is an instrument of divine communication. It can propose a
revelation for direction or condition us by our moral ideals. You
can have vision without being a visionary. Brave Vision speaks to
the Snellen 20/20 ideology and begs to differ that Vision is not an Eye experience
but an "I" experience, that both your heart and
mind have to be set before you can see from any angle, any
distance, from any perspective for anything. After this my prayer is that you can
look in the mirror at yourself and say I See Me because I Saw Him first.

BRAVE VISION

The methods describe within this book & or eBook are the author's personal thoughts

No part of this eBook may be reproduced or transmitted in any form or by any means, electronic or mechanical, including photocopying, recording or by any information storage and retrieval system, without written permission from the author

www.KhalilahOlokunola.com

Copyright © 2017 by Khalilah Olokunola
All rights reserved.

This book, Chapter or any portion thereof
may not be reproduced or used in any manner whatsoever
without the express written permission of the publisher
except for the use of brief quotations in a book review.
Printed in the United States of America

Publishing
THE WELL HEELED HUSTLE Publishing
www.TheWellHeeledHustle.com

Contact the Author
Khalilah@KhalilahOlokunola.com

For Booking
www.KhalilahOlokunola.com

Facebook
KhalilahEquips

Twitter
KhalilahEquips

Instagram
KhalilahEquips

Brave Lessons
Mondays at 8pm Est Via FB Live

You Tube Past Talks | Videos
Khalilah Olokunola

THANKS

I would like to take time out to thank some folks

First, I am ever grateful to God for giving me the vision, the strength and the endurance I needed to complete this assignment.

Thank you to my husband who has prayed me through and talked me through the past 16 years we have had together. You always gave your blessing when I wanted to work what I believe God was telling me to and you always supported it. I love you. You watched me work all kind of hours of the night rebuilding because I had fell to pieces. You encouraged me in seeing my worth even when I couldn't see it. You believed in me when I didn't believe in myself. Thank you for listening to section after section and giving me your honest opinion. You're the real MVP.

Thank you to my children Kairos' & Adam who showed patience with me when I had to work and couldn't play. For encouraging me to keep going even when I didn't feel like it. For slapping me high five when you saw I needed it and for praying me through when I was bed bound. And to Shamiya & Anastasia – I love you guys and am so proud of the young women you both have become, Thank you for just being you.

Thank you mom and dad for letting me hide away at your house to get a few pages done when I needed a quiet space that came with coffee, diet coke and good food.

Thank you to my sisters in the gospel Angela C. Gray & Yasira Sonnier for your support and prayers. We spent plenty days on the phone in prayer, in sharing but always in supporting. I am grateful for the cloud of witnesses that God has given me in these powerful women

Thank you to my Pastor Daniel Cook. I came to the Sanctuary of Wilmington at a difficult time. I had begun to walk in my old brokenness, my old disbelief. I was dwindling spiritually and no one heard or listened to my cry for help but the word you shared every week encouraged me to press, pursue, overcome, to fight and to believe again. I am stronger, I am more confident in who God created me to be and I am grateful that you decided to walk in Brave Vision and fulfill the assignment God gave you.

BRAVE Vision starts an early age. At an age when we can't define what it is we see or what it is we want but we recognize that there is something in front of us. If you had a chance to read the 1st workbook Be Brave, then you know that I realized that what I had in my earlier years was a goal and not a vision but let me tell you what happened before that and after.

As kids we see and look up to our parents, Firefighters, Police Officers, Doctors or the Guy on the corner slinging and decide based on what we perceive who we want to be. Khalilah wanted to become an attorney. At the age of 5. I knew how to present and how to make a case, especially when it came to advocating for Menudo or playing that Michael Jackson Vinyl on my record player that resembles a juke box over and over again. I was successful at it; my dad will vouch for me even though my mom frequently objected.

I won case after case for everything including debating in school or setting reasonable doubt why I received an 89 and not a 100 because B's were unacceptable in my house.

It wasn't until I started attending Yogi Bear Saturday Sunday School that my vision changed. I was interested in this God they talked about, interested in this God they worshipped. I would feel what some call goosebumps whenever I attended. And to this day I can still remember scoring 30 bucks for best dress for Halloween as May West with my homemade costume complete with Jeri Curl wig. It was the day Pastor Bill Wilson, known worldwide for Metro Kids told us that this God was our God!

We were always excited to attend, always excited to serve. It was fun learning about the bible and about our God week after week until one day outside of Pastor Bill Wilson's & David's office – Vanessa Cox who was my Missionettes leader

Brave Vision

(We learned scriptures for patches) prayed over me and asked that I would be filled with the Holy Spirit and something happened that to this day I can't explain but I wouldn't dare try.

What I will say is that I walked away with something outside of Snellen's 20/20 Vision. If you're not familiar with Snellen, his charts display letters of progressively smaller size. "Normal" vision is 20/20. This means that the test subject sees the same line of letters at 20 feet that a person with normal vision sees at 20 feet.

However, I began to see the world different. It wasn't good or bad but I now began to understand my nakedness. I understood what my Mom and Dad tried to shield us from, I understood why Yogi Bear picked up kids mostly in inner city neighborhoods and bought them to church every week. I understood why we had to move when bullets went through our window and through the wall we watched TV in front of. The world was far from picture perfect and it wasn't until after a little boy that lived up the block from me that I played with sometimes gave me a black eye over a toy that I realized that what you see despite the distance you're looking at it from; it may not be what you get. This was someone I played with, laughed with, shared my quarter waters and salt and vinegar chips with, Someone I would give my last box of Boston baked beans or Lemonheads to.

Running home crying for help made matters worse. My mom in all of her righteousness gave me that look that every child is familiar with and marched me back down the block only to tell me that if I didn't hit this little boy back that she would whip my behind. Back then there were switches & a wooden spoon that she called Mr. Do right and anything we did wrong it would make us do right.

All I could do was cry but the more I cried, the more I cringed and the more I cringed, the more I realized that Vision is never just about the Eyes but the I's.

One may see visions without being visionary. The Great men and women we read about in the bible that received visions were all individuals of action, individuals that provoked change. It is evident from any reading of their stories and the lives they lived that their assignments as Change Champions, their assignments as

Brave Vision

Kingdom Builders was supported and not stifled by the plausible cause that they had received a dispensation of vision at an appointed time in the purpose of God, from God and from the relationship they had with Him that started internally with a transformation.

A transformation similar to a metamorphosis where the caterpillar becomes a butterfly. A radical change in form, perception and ideas where both your heart and mind have to be transformed, before being set so that you can see from any angle, any distance, from any perspective for anything.

See, the big E at the top of Snellen's chart that was created in 1862 but has been modified since measures 20/200 vision so the ability to read that is said to be no big deal. It actually classifies an individual who can only see at that level as legally blind however I know and want you to understand that we all see things differently. At different levels, during different seasons and for different reasons.

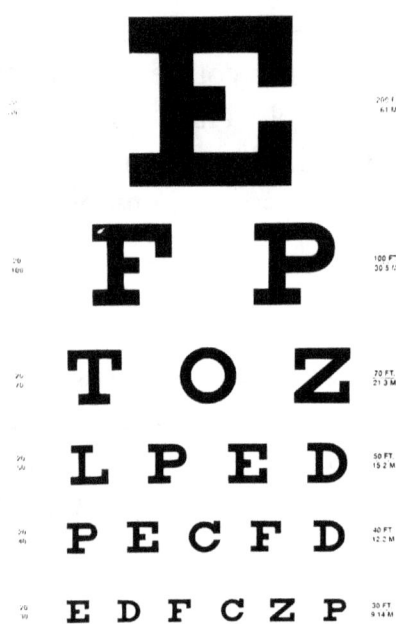

What if seeing the E was the goal? What if the E was what was assigned for those whose vision matches that capability and nothing more until their capabilities were increased?

You Have to see It, to build It

Brave Vision

What if we "looked" at things from a life perspective as opposed to a NOW perspective and understood that each one of us were made differentially to occupy pre-ordained opportunities made available to us. And that our circumstances, situations, struggles and strongholds play a role in shaping the vision that we need for the position we have been called to?

What if I told you that none us will ever see the same because our role in service is not the same and our perception is predicated on how we develop who we are and not what we see with the natural eye. The very thing you thought would break you, is what will make you and become the driving force of the foundational development you will need to build upon for your purpose driven life despite hurt, despite pain and despite fear. This is Brave Vision

And for young Khalilah, it was that moment standing between my mom and the little boy I called friend that changed my life forever. It was that moment that defined what I would do next, it was that moment the 1st stronghold took grip of my heart and my mind and I found myself barely in 5th grade trapped between fears; each of a different kind that would follow me, mock me and eventually immobilize me for the decades that were to come. And I didn't SEE it coming.

THE APPOINTMENT

The History & Symptoms Sheet

HISTORY

Everyone has a back story , A story that stresses what challenges we have overcome in our lives. A story that may cause others to quiver, cry , laugh or shake our heads at.

Each backstory is different and that is what makes us different . That is what sets us apart from the people we know. It is our story that helped shape us into who we are today . The story that does not begin with Once Upon A Time & may not have ended with a Happily Ever After . It is our story that will also set someone free .

Our history is similar to the textbooks we learned with in school about our nations forefathers, the laws that have been implemented and the challenges so many have encountered but what sets our story apart is that we have first hand knowledge through first hand accounts on the pain that we have experienced, the tears that we have shed and the results of the story that no one may never read about or hear but we carry around with us every day like that heavy text book we carried around in our book bags in school .

Brave Vision does not start where we are but began when we were born . Everything that led up into this moment, the right now is part of that heavy text book you carry. Denying the facts of it or not acknowledging it , is exactly why most of us have not arrived at the place we have so desired in life. Ignoring what was as if it could not possibly affect what is or what could be is the reason why I know, I understand and why I stand on the fact that Brave Vision is an I Thing not just an EYE thing .

HISTORY

It is an emotional disposition than defines a physical position.

A disposition meaning a person's inherent qualities of mind and character and a position meaning a place where someone or something is located or has been put.

You have been shaped by your history . You are molded and mended by the the predominant or prevailing tendency of your spirit; your natural mental and emotional outlook & mood. It has developed your characteristic attitude and planned your life to be what it is today. And the reason why you can not see yourself outside the scope of where you are , what people have told you, the title that you possess or the paycheck you bring in , is because the Optic Nerve that sends impulses & pictures seen by the eye to the brain from the retina so that it can be processed has been damaged by a history in hiding that affected both your heart & mind .

Your heart is the whole of the innermost part of the human, NOT merely the emotions. .

The Biblical word "heart," is the inner aspect of a man, made of three parts all together, with the primary part being the brain (the mind)

Those 3 parts include:

1) The Mental Process, which is the major part where action & reaction take place that leads a person in their life. These include perception, memory, thinking (such as ideation, imagination, belief, reasoning, etc.), volition, and emotion. Sometimes the term cognitive function is used instead.

HISTORY

It also includes :

2) Emotions which only process as reaction, as icing on the cake to either cultivate or impoverish our lives or . These despondancies, commotions and agitations all have names that we willfully express with emoticons . Silently hoping that someone will say something to make us feel better ab. Some include

Love
Passion
Pride
Sadness
Sentiment
Shame
Sympathy
Warmth
Fear

And finally
3) The Will, the seat of the will (discretionary, volitional, decision-making) where decisions are made between the rational and the emotional. Through what makes sense and what does not . God has a will for our lives but He also gave us "free will" which is the opportunity to make choices that genuinely affect our destiny. When we were created in Gods own image that included the ability to choose, Ask Eve .

However, free will should not mean and does not mean that we can do anything we want without causing a ripple effect in our own lives and the lives of others that we have surrounded ourselves with. Our choices should be based on what we morally value, what we believe is right and in line with what works best for who we have been created to be .

HISTORY

However it is difficult to make those right decisions when you no longer possess the ability to see . I know because I did it . I hid from the many backstories I experienced from birth up until now . It did shape me into who I am today but not without limitations and the fear that came along with it . Each scenario played a starring role in what I would do next. It changed my behavior , my ability to see right & wrong . Even worst it began to dictate what I felt about myself . See before the story I wanted to practice law, save lives, change the world but the the backstories I experienced took all of that away. Instead I saw brokenness , I saw hurt, I saw fear , I saw outrage , I saw a clueless victim being tormented day in and day out until I came to a point where I was numb and couldn't see anything at all . And as it is in the natural , Optic nerve damage can lead to vision distortion, vision loss, and blindness . I was there , I can diagnose myself now but back then I didn't understand the symptoms enough to realize that I needed a divine appointment with God .

HISTORY

Let's take a deep breath and look at our history. I started by mapping my timeline. I encourage you to do the same when you are alone or with a close friend or spouse.

First

Write down those things you have not been able to say out loud

Second

Create a Timeline of your life by writing down special moments & everything in between. Start from the earliest and work your way up to the present

Third

Pray the prayer written & insert your name in it

Fourth

Make an intentional appointment with God

HISTORY

The Power of Words

1. Pray 1st: God give me the strength to release those things I must let go from my history & my present so that I can see. Forgive me & help me to forgive those that hurt me. Shift my words from pain to power so that what I say will line up with your word.

2. Write down those things that you have not been able to say out Loud

3. Declare: I am fearfuly & wonderfully made

4. Think about everything you ever wanted to say to those that hurt you. Write them a letter. Remember this is your chance to be as expressive as you want

5. Pray Last: God Thank you for your Grace. Your Direction, Your Strength & the ability to forgive myself & others that have hurt me

Brave
VISION

HISTORY

Write down those things that you have not been able to say out Loud

Follow the steps so that you do not overwhelm yourself - Taking

breaks in between . Here's what my first entry looked like for me

on day 1

So I prayed today & asked God to help me get past the hurt of
the past and the present but I found myself angry at a lot of

people including
myself . I wanted to say No all those times but I was afraid . I didnt

really want to hang out with that crowd but I wanted someone to
love me

to make me feel like I was special ....at least sometimes.
I disliked the old Khalilah but I also love her.

Brave
VISION

History

History

HISTORY

Brave
VISION

History

History

History

Brave
VISION

History

History

History

History

HISTORY

History

I'm not sure how far you have gotten into writing down everything that you have been hiding.

The Challenge is always admitting that we have played a role in where we are and will play a role in where we want to go. In the first workbook BE BRAVE, we learned in A to accept responsibility, to become more accountable of our actions and lack there of.

Even though our backstories have a way of crippling us from moving forward, in the press is where we find breakthrough.

Press is an action word and that means that we can not:

Stand still and press
Lie still and press
Wait still and press or
Cry still and press.

We have to arise from that dark place, that dead place like Lazarus and come forth. Not only for ourselves but the bible is clear when it says many came to see what Jesus had done and grew faith in him and that means that in anything we do whether it is your career, your business or your life some one elses faith to believe the inevitable, the impossible and the miraculous is tied to you coming out of your grave.

Are you still with me?

Tracking a timeline of your life is not to kick up your mess but to search for the root, the unanswered questions that lie in wait so that the damage youve encountered can be healed

Brave Vision

Brave
VISION
TIMELINE

If you're not ready to create a timeline go to The "I" Chart Chapter

You Have to see It, to build It

Brave Vision

Brave
VISION
TIMELINE

If you're not ready to create a timeline go to The "I" Chart Chapter

You Have to see It, to build It

Brave Vision

Brave
VISION
TIMELINE

If you're not ready to create a timeline go to The "I" Chart Chapter

You Have to see It, to build It

Brave VISION TIMELINE

If you're not ready to create a timeline go to The "I" Chart Chapter

Brave VISION TIMELINE

If you're not ready to create a timeline go to The "I" Chart Chapter

Brave VISION TIMELINE

If you're not ready to create a timeline go to The "I" Chart Chapter

Brave VISION TIMELINE

If you're not ready to create a timeline go to The "I" Chart Chapter

Brave VISION TIMELINE

If you're not ready to create a timeline go to The "I" Chart Chapter

THE SYMPTOMS

HOW DO YOU KNOW THAT YOU HAVE LOST YOUR ABILITY TO SEE

Brave Vision

Brave
VISION
IMPAIRED

What are some of the symptoms

SYMPTOMS

Pain - SURFACE
HAVE YOU BEEN HURT?

Sensitivity - PENETRATION
ARE YOU OVERLY SENSITIVE?

Numbness - ESTABLISHMENT
DO YOU SAY I DONT CARE?

Tingling or prickling - CULTIVATED
EVERY LITTLE THING ANNOYS YOU

Problems with positional awareness - ACCEPTED
YOU DONT UNDERSTAND YOUR VALUE

Jealousy - REACTIVE SYMPTOM
YOU GET UPSET WHEN OTHER PEOPLE ARE BLESSED

Persistent sadness - REACTIVE SYMPTOM
NOTHING SEEMS TO MAKE YOU HAPPY

Feelings of hopelessness and helplessness.
YOU DONT FEEL LIKE THERE IS ANYTHING LEFT OR ANYONE TO HELP

Thoughts of death or even suicide.
IF YOU ANSWERED YES HERE CALL 911 OR CALL US.

Increased agitation, irritability and anxiety
EVERYTHING BOTHERS YOU

BLINDNESS

| PAIN SURFACE | PAIN UNADDRESSED CAUSES PENETRATION | PAIN ESTABLISHED CAUSES VISUAL DISTORTION | PAIN CULTIVATED CAUSES VISUAL LOSS | PAIN ACCEPTED CAUSES BLINDNESS |

You Have to see It, to build It

Brave VISION IMPAIRED

SYMPTOM QUESTIONS
SYMPTOMS

✓ Have you been hurt before?

_____
_____
_____
_____
_____
_____

✓ Are You still hurting today? If you Answered yes then continue If you Answered No head over to Chapter 2 The "I" Chart

_____
_____
_____
_____
_____
_____

✓ Has the pain gone unaddressed | has it established | has it been cultivated and did you accept it ?

_____
_____
_____
_____
_____
_____

You Have to see It, to build It

Brave VISION IMPAIRED

SYMPTOM QUESTIONS
SYMPTOMS

✓ Based on your timeline, can you see where it started?

_____
_____
_____
_____
_____
_____
_____

✓ Are You ready to address the pain and repair the impairment to your vision?

_____
_____
_____
_____
_____
_____
_____

Pray this prayer

God I thank you for meeting me where I am, I thank you for who you are and I thank you for where I am going in you. God I pray for a divine appointment in my life where you uproot, tear down, burn down and blow away the ashes of any pain & hurt that has taken root in my spirit, in my house and in my life. I declare I will be like the dry bones in Ezekial when you are finished - where there is no evidence of my flesh and that you would breath fresh winds of new life upon me right now so that I can live in you. In Jesus Name I pray - AMEN

Brave Vision

THE APPOINTMENT

A divine appointment is a meeting that has been unmistakably ordered by God to steer us towards His path in our purpose. And Today is your day.

God can and will often use some of the inconveniences & broken moments in our life for breakthrough to set us up for a divine appointment.

The Bible says in

Psalms 37:23

The Steps of A Good Man are ordered by the Lord & He delights in his way This is A Psalm of David that begins in verse 1 with the words : Fret not thyself because of evildoers, neither be thou envious against the workers of iniquity.

This scripture is saying it doesn't matter what the world does or what wickedness you have surrounded yourself with. Your pace, your processional in life - You Good man | Good woman : You warrior with the strength and ability to fight is pre ordained and orchestrated by God who takes pleasure in bending your will to his . The Good man , You and I may fall and God may order or allow this to happen but he will still guide us in all truth because no matter how many times we fall , we are still his - We are complete in Him without spot or blemish .

Brave Vision — THE APPOINTMENT

We remain as Kings kids, called of a royal priesthood . If you look back at your timeline you will realize that it may have hurt but you made it to this pivotal point in your life and that is because of your appointment with God. . Let me explain

In Acts 10, Peter was sent to the house of Cornelius. In John 4, Jesus met the woman at Sychar's well.......

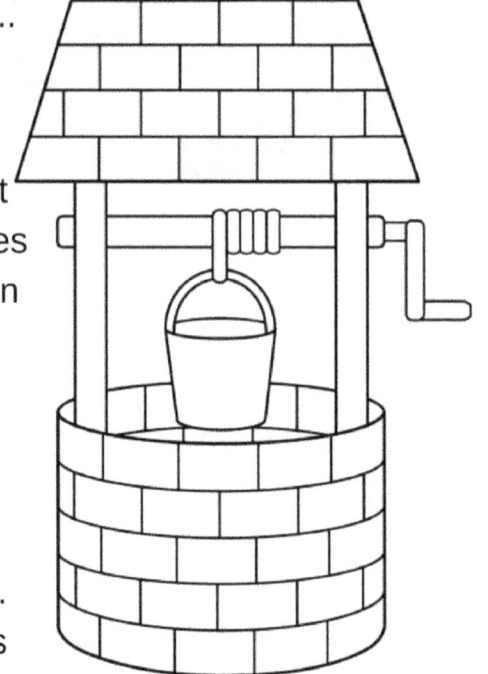

I remember forgetting for the entire day that I had to go to the grocery store and when I finally remembered it was dark but I went anyway . I walked through the aisles and ran into a young lady I haven't seen in a long time and she burst into tears while saying she had been asking God to send someone to encourage her . And if you know me , you know that I am always ready to do just that . We prayed right there in Aisle 8 at the local Harris Teeter . I never looked at aisle 8 the same . It was on that day that I realized that we are always on assignment no matter what we are going through . Someone may be praying for help and you may be the help that they have been praying for.

It is the divine appointments in our lives with God or orchestrated by God that serve as the genesis to our New beginnings .

Brave Vision — THE APPOINTMENT

Rahab's genesis was a divine appointment with the two spies that she hid under the flax which went unnoticeable because it was the SEASON of the barley harvest and the flax was expectd to be lying to dry. The spies simply told her to add a scarlet cord to her window . That scarlet cord is a freedom symbol that we see modernized in the red light district to say I am here but for Rahab she was SAYING OUT LOUD I know who I am , I know what I have done but I know that the LORD has given this land to you and that a great fear of you has fallen on us, so that all who live in this country are melting in fear because of you. Now then, please swear to me by the LORD that you will show kindness to my family, because I have shown kindness to you. Give me A SURE SIGN that you will spare the lives of my father and mother, my brothers and sisters, and all who belong to them, and that you will save us from death.

That Divine appointment shifted her entire family and the generations to come and all she did was say Yes.

Divine Appointment are only orchestrated by God | in God & a vessel
Divine Appointments always happen at the right time , during the right season
Divine Appointments often require an honest declaration to God
Divine Appointments will always have a sure sign that confirms .
Divine Appointments can bring change for generations to come

I have had many **DIVINE APPOINTMENTS** in my life but because of my history I suffered from reactive emotions that were displayed in bad behaviors. The saying Hurt people, hurt people is a fact. I couldn't see the opportunities that God had presented me in any area of my life because I didn't acknowledge or accept the symptoms associated with my loss of vision. I had allowed the replays of the assaults I had encountered when I was a child by my babysitter| family members and people I thought were friends to replay over and over again. All I heard was the screaming, the arguing, the fights, the brokenness, the repeat offenses that escalated until I was numb. And all I could remember was the penetration of heart and mind that made some of these childhood happenings become my new normal.

I hid my pain well – I continued to make Straight A's, grab awards, jump on the deans lists and still participate in extra-curricular activities because what once hurt was shaping me into becoming someone other than who God called me to be until I couldn't hide it anymore.

My parents increased my insurance policy because they thought I was going to be killed in the streets, my mom called the G building because she thought I had lost my mind – She was correct and my dad just wanted me out the house.

I eventually took in an overnight at The G building (known as the place for people with mental illness) – My mom had the cops pick me up and take me there and it broke me a little bit but it was being put out as a teenager and forced to ride the trains from Canarsie to Manhattan all night that shook me a little.

I didn't have anywhere to go. I stayed at friend's houses here and there but it was never long term. And anyone that offered long term needed collateral for my stay and the collateral they wanted was my body, something I refused to give up at this point.

I would weep on nights when it was colder than usual | nights I was more exhausted than usual or those moments when my stomach would growl and I didn't have anything to put in it. I was 15. I felt alone and couldn't see any hope in any part of my life but despite the clash of emotions I faced and the battle that I knew would lie ahead, the brokenness I called my life prequalified me as the perfect candidate for a Divine Appointment. And Even though I could not see it, one was on the way.

Have you ever been in a place where you were so broken you couldn't feel?

Yes	No	I'm Not Sure

Do you understand the escalation of the symptoms now? Can you Identify them?

Yes	No	I'm Not Sure

Can you pin point a place in time where God orchestrated a Divine Appointment?

Yes	No	I'm Not Sure

The "I" Exam vs The "Eye" Exam

A SERIES OF TESTS THAT MEASURE A PERSON'S OCULAR & INTERNAL HEALTH AND VISUAL STATUS FOR THE ABILITY TO SEE

Brave Vision

There is no real way to measure who you are in front of people as opposed to who you are in the privacy of your own home when the secret of the I versus the eye lies on the inside of you. In that place you decided a long time ago to let anyone enter again.

We run from, we hide hurt and pain by covering it up with whatever is convenient and easy at the time. For some the cover up is with drugs, alcohol, food, shopping but for others its inappropriate behaviors, relationships where you find that you have lowered your standard and a place where you have lost your ability to say No.

For a long time, my I am's were very different from my I See's.

I would always proudly say I am followed by some power word proudly topped off by a high five to whomever I was speaking to but my reality was that I did not truly believe anything that I said. I wasn't vested in who I said I was but instead in what I saw when I looked in the mirror when no one was around. I saw a woman who had been scorned | broken| hurt | offended | let down | disappointed | abused | assaulted | disrespected | ignored | neglected | objectified | taunted | not as attractive as everyone else and not as smart as everyone else.

These words piled on my heart and my mind created a picture that only I saw that was contrary to what I said.

I know now that I disliked who I was and it was evident by my inability to forgive myself for the mistakes I made and for the hurt that others incurred upon me that I blamed myself for to.

I knew that I had to turn things around if I wanted to live but how in the world would I ask for help and who could I allow inside of the place I had closed off for so long for the support I began to realize I needed.

I am not sure where you are today but because you have this workbook I am convinced that you desire to tap into a new level of vision for your life | your business | your career | your relationship.

I know that the measurement of our ocular and internal health can limit our effectiveness in everything connected to who we are. We never read about someone being given the gift of vision in the bible but instead it is given during a

Brave Vision

specific season of their lives for the task ahead that they have to encounter, serve in or birth for the Kingdom of God.

That **REVELATION** tells me that when we can **SEE** – we have been **ACTIVATED.**

Activation according to Merriam's dictionary **means** to set up or formally institute (as a military unit) with the necessary personnel and equipment. **God will send you who need and give you what you need for the road ahead**

The *(2) second definition is*: to put (an individual or unit) on active duty – **God will position you for the work that He predestined and foreknew for you before the foundation of this world**

Now think about the credit card process when you activate a new card. Before you receive it, you have to meet the qualifications and only when you qualify do they ship the card with the limit you have pre-qualified for.

The I versus the Eye for Brave Vision is when your past has prequalified you for use by God. You have reached a peak where you tap into the aptitude to detect, examine, identify and see the root of the issues that have plagued you for so long. It's at the point where you decide that your I AM and Your I See is intertwined and that in order to press into your full potential in your life you have to believe that the veil has been torn. You have to allow the word of God to cloud what you once saw so that your new discerning mind can distinguish without difficulty by sight or with the other senses that you are who God says you are in all aspects.

It was at this point in my life that I knew that in order to tap into my God given potential I would have to go back into my personal pit in order to come forward to take my position in the palace.

I would have to revisit the hurt and the pain I once experienced in order to tap into the joy that was waiting for me.

Listen, **there is absolutely no way that you can build it big in your business, your career or in your life – If your life Is a hidden mess.**

I am a firm believer that without being personally well, you cannot be a professional success. By taking charge of your personal development we can begin to facilitate positive progress for your professional development that creates fruit that you can see. You do want to see the fruit don't you?

I know it's difficult especially when everyone surrounding you or at the least the ones you see online appear to be super successful with no cares in the world. They seem to have a picture perfect life that many would covet, however I want you to remember in moving forward that the I See is not always the I Am! Here is what I realized………

The most detrimental and lasting solutions to some of our problems offer the potential to **save others** from facing the same dilemma, dramatically **improving their ability** to succeed and **strengthening your own confidence and trust in the performance of the promises of God** for your life.

My Brave Vision & yours is not just about us, it's about those who our vision is connected to and those our vision will impact.

If you are ready for breakthrough – You are ready for the "I" Opener

SCAN THE QR CODE FIRST FOR A WORD FROM ME

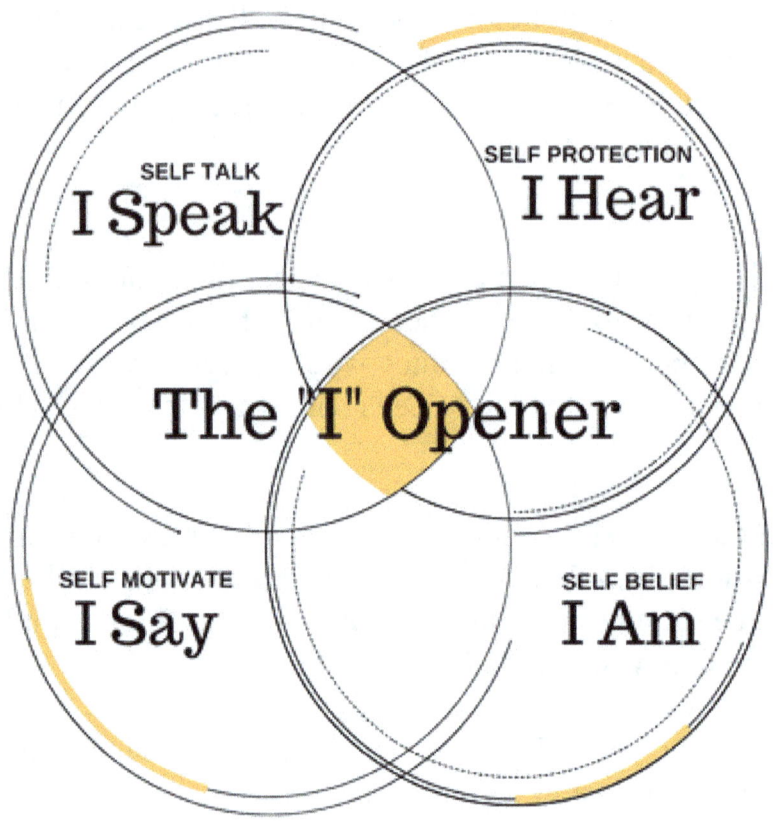

DAILY "I" OPENER

Statistics say that it takes 21 days to develop a habit – 72 hours to break one so for the next 21 days:

1st –Make this part of your daily declaration | affirmation and motivation
I SAY | I SPEAK | I HEAR, THEREFORE I AM
CUSTOMIZE IT TO MAKE IT YOUR OWN

HERE'S MINE
I SAY I CAN DO ALL THINGS
I SPEAK PEACE INTO MY LIFE
I DECIDE TO HEAR ONLY WHAT IS IT GOOD FOR ME
I AM BRAVE

Brave Vision

2ⁿᵈ - USE THE I AM SHEETS TO REMIND YOURSELF OF WHO YOU ARE. Choose 1 word and insert it on each line

3ʳᵈ – Begin to write the vision of what you see now

BRAVE VISION

I am

I AM

I AM

I Am

> Brave

> Powerful

> Strong

> Smart

WHAT WORDS CAN YOU ADD TO DESCRIBE YOU

You Have to see It, to build It

BRAVE VISION

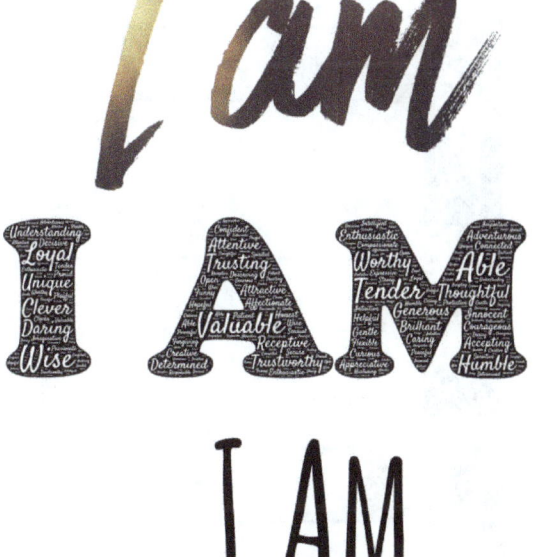

I AM

I Am

> _____
> _____
> _____
> _____
> _____

WHAT WORDS CAN YOU ADD TO DESCRIBE YOU

BRAVE VISION

I am

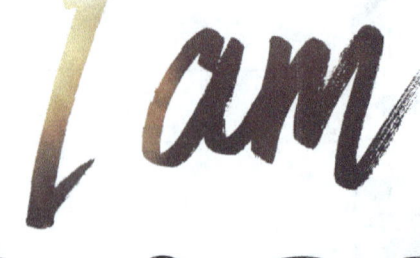

I AM

I Am

› _____

› _____

› _____

› _____

WHAT WORDS CAN YOU ADD TO DESCRIBE YOU

BRAVE VISION

I am

I AM

I Am

> _____
> _____
> _____
> _____
> _____

WHAT WORDS CAN YOU ADD TO DESCRIBE YOU

BRAVE VISION

_____

_____

_____

_____

WHAT WORDS CAN YOU ADD TO DESCRIBE YOU

You Have to see It, to build It

BRAVE VISION

I am

I AM

I Am

> _____
> _____
> _____
> _____
> _____

WHAT WORDS CAN YOU ADD TO DESCRIBE YOU

What is your final I AM?

This is the word that you begin your journey with. The one word that will set the course of the vision that you are preparing to rewrite for your business, your career and your life.

How does that one word make you feel? Are you confident enough to say it in front of others?

If you answered yes, your 20/20 Is on the horizon. If you answered no, I want you to go back to **PAGE 14 – THE POWER OF WORDS** and **SAY| SPEAK| HEAR:**
POINT 1 – THE PRAYER

The Damascus Refraction

Receiving Your Prescription to See

Brave Vision

Before his conversion, Paul, then known as Saul, was a "zealous" Pharisee who Intensely persecuted the followers of Jesus. Says Paul in his Epistle to the Galatians:

For you have heard of my previous way of life in Judaism, how intensely I persecuted the church of God and tried to destroy it. I was advancing in Judaism beyond many of my own age among my people and was extremely zealous for the traditions of my fathers.
— Galatians 1:13–14, NIV

In the First Epistle to the Corinthians describes Paul his conversion as having seen the risen Christ:

For what I received I passed on to you as of first importance: that Christ died for our sins according to the Scriptures, that he was buried, that he was raised on the third day according to the Scriptures, and that he appeared to Cephas, and then to the Twelve. After that, he appeared to more than five hundred of the brothers and sisters at the same time, most of whom are still living, though some have fallen asleep. Then he appeared to James, then to all the apostles, and last of all he appeared to me also, as to one abnormally born.
— 1 Cor. 15:3–8, NIV

The Epistle to the Galatians also describes his conversion as a divine revelation, with Jesus appearing to Paul.

I want you to know, brothers and sisters, that the gospel I preached is not of human origin. I did not receive it from any man, nor was I taught it; rather, I received it by revelation from Jesus Christ. For you have heard of my previous way of life in Judaism, how intensely I persecuted the church of God and tried to destroy it. I was advancing in Judaism beyond many of my own age among my people and was extremely zealous for the traditions of my fathers. But when God, who set me apart from my mother's womb and called me by his grace, was pleased to reveal his Son in me so that I might preach him among the Gentiles, my immediate response was not to consult any human being.
— Galatians 1:11-16, NIV

Brave Vision

In the book of Acts, it presents the conversion experience in far more detail than in the previous accounts we have noted.

The Book of Acts says that Paul was on his way from Jerusalem to Damascus to seek out and arrest followers of Jesus, with the intention of returning them to Jerusalem as prisoners for questioning and possible execution . This is the same Paul named Saul at the time who was present during the stoning of Stephen.

While on the road to Damascus Paul sees a light from heaven flash around him. He fell to the ground and heard a voice say to him, "Saul, Saul, why do you persecute me?"

"Who are you, Lord?" Saul asked.

"I am Jesus, whom you are persecuting," he replied. "Now get up and go into the city, and you will be told what you must do."

The men traveling with Saul stood there speechless; they heard the sound but did not see anyone. Saul got up from the ground, but when he opened his eyes he could see nothing. So they led him by the hand into Damascus. For three days he was blind, and did not eat or drink anything.
— Acts 9:3–9, NIV

The scripture continues with a description of Ananias of Damascus receiving a word from the Lord instructing him to visit Saul at the house of Judas on the Street Called Straight and to lay hands on him to restore his sight. Ananias response is for another book but let's just say that because he had "HEARD" about Saul's persecution he was reluctant but obeys the command of God anyhow.

QUESTION: How Many of us try to give God our opinion when He wants to use us to restore someone He has called because of what we have HEARD?

"Lord," Ananias answered, "I have heard many reports about this man and all the harm he has done to your holy people in Jerusalem. And he has come here with authority from the chief priests to arrest all who call on your name."

You Have to see It, to build It

**But the Lord said to Ananias, "Go! This man is my chosen instrument to proclaim my name to the Gentiles and their kings and to the people of Israel. I will show him how much he must suffer for my name."
Then Ananias went to the house and entered it. Placing his hands on Saul, he said, "Brother Saul, the Lord—Jesus, who appeared to you on the road as you were coming here—has sent me so that you may see again and be filled with the Holy Spirit." Immediately, something like scales fell from Saul's eyes, and he could see again. He got up and was baptized, and after taking some food, he regained his strength and preached Christ Straightway.
— Acts 9:13–19, NIV**

Let's look at the text. Scripture says that the men traveling with Saul Heard a sound but did not see anyone

The word Heard can be translated as both Hear and understand. This is a noun in the accusative and with the use of the accusative it indicates hearing with understanding. This means that Saul's companions may have heard the voice but could not understand it. They could not comprehend enough to receive a glimpse of the Glory that was specific to Paul on the road to Damascus.

On this journey to Brave Vision the Damascus Refraction represents the final straw | The Last time you walk blindly. The place where you ask God, what is it you will have me to do. It is your ultimate Divine Appointment, an encounter of the highest kind that penetrate every area that once held you bound so that you can begin the process of being able to see.
 It is the place where your past receives a stop sign and the only way forward is in God and not everyone can come with you.

Similar to a refraction of sound or of light there is a bending that is adjusted to your will. Some things will pass by and through others that only you will be able to hear, see and receive.

Refraction is the phenomenon which makes image formation possible by the eye

The refraction test is notably an eye exam that measures a person's prescription for eyeglasses or contact lenses.

See, when there is a refraction of light or sound, it bends & changes direction when it goes from one medium to another. An example is from Air to Water. The depth and height are all taken into accountability for the reception of what you see and in this case what you hear.

The process of vision begins when light rays that reflect off objects and travel through the eye's optical system are refracted and focused into a point of sharp focus, this according to health line.

You will have friends that cannot understand, co-workers who cannot understand, family members who cannot understand. And what you have to come to terms with is this fact:

Your Prescription to see is handwritten with your name on it. It is for you, and you alone. When a doctor prescribes a prescription it is based on your history, symptoms and diagnosis - God does the same.

I could shout right there – Did you catch that?

Brave Vision started with your:
History | Your Symptoms | Your Diagnosis | Your Divine Appointment & Now Your Damascus Refraction to receive your Prescription to SEE.

I know you are still asking yourself, why didn't the companions hear? That answer is the Key

God is the only one who can repair your impaired vision, the only one who can remove the scales from your eyes by giving another vision to a reluctant subject to lay hands on you so that you can have your vision restored.

And there was a certain disciple at Damascus, named Ananias; and to him said the Lord in a vision, Ananias. And he said, Behold, I *am here*, Lord. Acts 9:11

It will be a suddenly, an immediately, an even now experience for your life.

Don't be surprised if God uses someone who has "Heard" about you to set you free.

Remember Jesus is the carpenter, Carpenters can remove walls and build doors compatible to the structure they are working on.

There is a wall that needs to come down that is obscuring your vision to see and God is going to put a few windows and an open door for you to view the green grass, the fully bloomed flowers and the trees that bare the fruit you thought was not there. **See it! If you can keep going. If you cannot, Head back to page 29 and review your history and see how far you have come.**

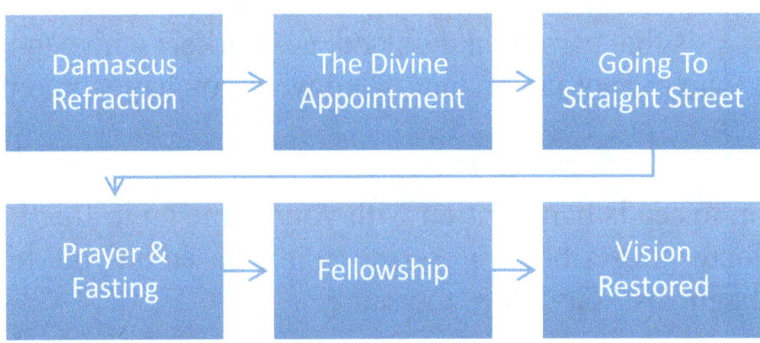

I hope that you were able to move forward and not head back to your history. You have come a long way since you started your journey to BRAVE VISION. To finally seeing God for who He is in your life and who you are to him!

And Now that God has your attention He desires for you to write the vision, write what you see for your Life, your business or career.

Writing the Vision in Habakkuk 2 the bible says to Write the Vision and Make It Plain although it tarry, wait for it, it will come. According to Bensons Commentary *the Lord said, Write the vision* — Write down what I am going to say. Every divine communication, by whatever means made, and it is often spoken of in the prophetic writings under the title of a *vision.* When the prophets were commanded to *write* anything, it denoted the great importance of it, and that the fulfilling of it was at some distance.

Creating a vision is an important part of your life. Creating a Brave Vision after experiencing the happenings of life is pivotal to your beginning again, understanding that the vision you create may not be expedited but may take time to manifest.

In 2006 I relocated to Wilmington NC to be married and I still recall the mindset I had when I made the move. All I wanted was to serve in the Kingdom, all I wanted was to minister the gospel. It was a word that had been given to me by a prophet, it was something that I saw but a decade later there had been a switch. I was not the Minister of the Gospel – I became known as the event girl who ministered sometimes and I wondered how I got there.

I blamed the lack of opportunity for my lack of results but today I realized that I was also to blame. Even though I felt rejected because there were no immediate opportunities the reality is that others cannot see what you see. They may not be capable of it.

Their mind and heart may be fixed to only identify the E at 20/200 when God has called you to 20/20 in Him.

Each day that past I became more and more engulfed in the lack of confidence I had and I stopped seeing past my current situation. I began to walk in the unbelief of what I use to believe. I allowed that vision loss to cultivate and because I was not able to identify the symptoms associated with blindness because I didn't understand **VISION**, my reactive emotions progressed. They progressed from anger to hurt, from hurt to pain, from pain to brokenness, from brokenness to bound and from bound to blind.

I showed out by building a business I grew to love but not loving the woman that was building the business. Khalilah was missing in action. There was something that I arrived with, that I no longer had. I searched in bars over too many glasses of Pinot Grigio and cigars dipped in bourbon at boogie events I was proud to attend. But when the lights went out and I was alone I would still see what was supposed to be like a bad dream that I could not wake up out of. The tears would fall until it was time to go out again or book the next event.

I was on TV, featured in print locally, regionally, nationally and internationally. I was designing looks for front covers of notable magazines, working on notable events and with a celebrity clientele. When I showed up people knew my name and it looked good from the outside looking in but it felt the opposite from the inside looking out. I wasn't happy with engulfing myself in the flashing lights of success while not fully walking in what was burning on the inside.

A burning that I was blind to. Have you been there. Have you operated in a place of convenience instead of a place of purpose and even though it felt good and looked good sometimes, it still hurt?

When God spoke to me about "Changing My Story" – He didn't use those words – He said a sunset was coming on the business I built from nothing and I knew that I couldn't be hearing right. But I was. Everything I booked after that came with drama attached that I had never seen before. I even landed a few appointments in court over it – Can I be Honest? Fortunately, I won those cases, I knew I would but the process destroyed me. It filled me with shame and anxiety. Even though many people didn't know I did and I walked around like I had a sign plastered on my front chest. I elevated the situation to beyond where it was and began to walk in shame, anxiety, depression and guilt. I was already blinded but now my other senses had been immobilized.

Days and weeks went by and I didn't know what to do. I didn't have a plan B in place but I did have that burning sensation of something more, of something greater that was coming.
I knew everyone but lacked a cloud of witnesses that could rally around me to pray me through. The people I saw daily and weekly although they would greet me with a hug or a holy kiss their intentions were not all whole.

I knew that some talked about me, some was overly jealous and others just didn't like me. I wondered if it was something that I had done and began asking God to show me, me!

I began being intentional with where I went and who I went with. I started praying more, worshipping more. When you are broken like Hannah was broken when she was provoked by her adversary Penninah in the bible you often find yourself at Shiloh. The place where you cry out to God to move and hope with the speck of faith you have left that He has heard your war cry.

Gods voice got louder and I finally came to terms with the fact that it was time for me to walk away so I did but I did it kicking and screaming. Letting go of anything is extremely difficult and I found myself displaced from a place I thought I belonged

What would it feel like not to be the "Event Girl"?
I was about to find out………

Brave Vision

I was sort of stuck and had no idea how I was going to get out but there was another appointment coming. Through journaling and creating action sheets for myself I gave birth to the 1st workbook Be Brave but what God did afterwards blew my mind.

I started sharing my heart and time with other women to help them along the way. I shared my mistakes, my shortcomings, my failures and a very few of my successes. I began receiving speaking engagement requests and even planned a book signing.

I asked myself what is the plan now and I didn't know but I remembered the vision I had when I was young, the words that had been spoken over my life, the feelings I had when I moved down here and that desire, that fire, that burning sensation on the inside of me began to speak and it said: Write what you see | Write the Vision.

To write a vision, you have to know what a vision is.

Vision is divine communication.

Vision is the faculty or state of being able to see

Vision is the act or power of sensing with the eyes

Vision is a manifestation to the senses of something immaterial

Vision is a projection of your intentions and what you perceive to see in your heart and mind. You should be able to sum it up in a few sentences with a statement and then describe it in detail.

Vision is not a HOW – It is a Why

To start you have to identify your core values, the things that get you excited and what do you believe you are called to and what do you want to see manifest in your life

Your vision is based on your own moral compass. What you believe and what you do not. What is your right and what is your wrong? It should be a projection of what you believe God will manifest.

This process is not individual to just your life but the structure of it can be used for your business | your career | your relationship & your finances.

The vision should have identifiable actionable goals that you need to accomplish in order to walk, work and birth the vision you write. It should be connected to & embedded in your heart so that even during a storm you will not be moved. It is a process but one that we start today together here at the Damascus Refraction. Here is the process but go get your groundbreaking tools first.

The Building Tools

THE SHOVEL | THE SEEDS | THE TRASH BAG

Building tools in any construction or reconstruction process are matched to the task. It is the specific needs required to perform the job successfully. You would not use a hammer for a screw and if you did – It might take you a bit longer to achieve the results you want. You would not wear glasses for 20/60 vision if your prescription is 20/100. It would be a strain | It would not perform the corrective measures required to strengthen the eye and you still wouldn't be able to see. Did you catch that? Without the right building tools, the right foundation, the right timing, the right state of mind & heart your process could be delayed and God wants to expedite the time you lost in your blind state. He wants to restore the years that were taken.

God will always meet us where we are but he is not a magician and he does not perform tricks. There are some things that we have to take ownership & do ourselves. It's similar to adding your name to a deed or a car title. That thing belongs to you and when it needs fixed you take it to the mechanic who is skilled for the need. Our development and ability to grow is a joint partnership. A partnership that is legal binding – We agree to walk in what it is we see | We agree to stand in midst of how we feel | We agree to challenge ourselves to begin again even when we could not see an exit sign or entry arrow along the way.

This section was the most difficult for me. I always work myself through the workbooks I produce for you 1st and I had a hard time digging deep| investing in myself and walking away from people and things. I spent hours in the car going back to situations I wanted to forget, I struggled with doing things for me that would make me feel good and I struggled with walking away without explanation from some people I called friend. However, this is what I learned – There are some things required of us that will not feel good, it will look even worst but they will end good.

I am sure Paul didn't like being confronted with himself but it ended good
I am sure Peter was afraid to get out the boat and walk on water but it ended good.
I am sure that the woman with the issue of blood didn't like crawling through the crowd but she used what she had, to get what she needed and it ended good.

Brave Vision

The Shovel - There are many types of shovels shaped and created differently for a specific task. A general category of shovels is tailored to digging hard ground that must be broken with substantial force before it can be moved.

Beginning to write your vision requires some deep digging where you will discover some of the answers to the questions you have for yourself for your life. Some of those answers you already have from the previous sections in the workbook but as you move forward into Brave Vision remember that your answers are for you and they should be honest | direct | to the point and intentional in discovery.

The Seeds - This is the investable in who you are and what you are going to do to achieve whatever success is defined for you in your business| your career | your relationships | your finances and your life. Seeds are where you start. It will be what you plant, what will be watered and what you will see the fruits of bloom.

The Trash Bags – We all have baggage and there's some things that we have to get rid of in our life before we begin writing the vision God allowed us to see.

The Be Brave 5 Point formula applies here.
1. Who are you surrounding yourself with and why?
2. Who are you?
3. Are you ready to accept responsibility for the backend and upfront for what you do from this point forth?
4. Are you prepared to venture outside of your box?
5. Do you expect to Win in God?

You Have to see It, to build It

Immediately following Saul's encounter on the road to Damascus the bible says that He:

1. Went to the house of Judas where he was told to wait – He surrounded himself with who God specified
2. He spent time in prayer and in fasting with himself and only God. I can only think about what was going through his mind after all the persecution he had done by his own hands. Saul had time to speak to God, time to think about himself, who he was and the responsibility that he had to accept for everything that happened before Damascus.
3. He was met by a man named Ananias who laid hands on him on Straight Street which can denote a new walk in and with God
4. After the scales from his eyes he saw things differently not through the EYES but the "I". His heart had experienced a direct divine encounter with God and this new life was now real in Him and He could see it. He no longer would live in the box of zealousness where he was deceived by the enemy.
5. Paul went straightway and preached the gospel. He believed it. he expected to win and knew that he could only do that with God

- It is okay to get rid of the toxic people in your life. Pack them a to go plate and learn to love them from far away.
- It is okay to separate yourself from anything that is familiar and kicks up your stuff. And when I say stuff I mean your old mindset | old behaviors | old ways. This can include People | Places & Things.
- Now go Grab a piece of paper &write down everything you can think off from the past 2 points. The toxic people, where & who you need to separate from and add this "The Old "YOUR NAME" is gone. Once you do that crumble it up and put that in your trash bag to.

Did that feel liberating. Do you feel fired up about where you are going? I hope so because God has purposed to take you places and it starts with

FIRST LET'S WRITE THE VISION STATEMENTS

REMEMBER YOUR VISION STATEMENT IS YOUR WHY

If you need help understanding what a vision statement is go back to the Damascus refraction

VISION STATEMENT FOR MY BUSINESS	
VISION STATEMENT FOR MY CAREER	
VISION STATEMENT FOR MY RELATIONSHIP	
VISION STATEMENT FOR MY FINANCES	
VISION STATEMENT FOR MY LIFE	
VISION STATEMENT FOR	
VISION STATEMENT FOR	

Now write what you see for your life right

MY VISION
Where there is no vision the people perish Proverbs 29:18
After You Write the Vision | You Map the Vision

_____
_____
_____
_____
_____
_____
_____
_____
_____
_____
_____
_____
_____
_____

Brave
VISION

Writing the Vision is a feel good experience but the vision we write, that we say we see requires work to achieve it. Our next step is mapping. This is when you create an actionable strategy that includes both the goals and tasks you need to achieve that vision. And remember it won't happen overnight but if you will work it, it will work.

GOALS TO GET THERE

Your Goals should be based on your vision statement and the areas you listed. Write down each goal based on that vision statement in the box.

Here's an example

VISION – Write a small book of inspiration in 90 days

⬇

GOAL – Pinpoint what type of inspiration it will be. Decide on print or E-book

⬇

Actionable task - Write 2 times a day | Price Book & E-book | Look for templates of similar books | Join author groups

Here's what happens

Actionable task ⟶ Goal ⟶ Vision

Does this make sense? Let's get you started

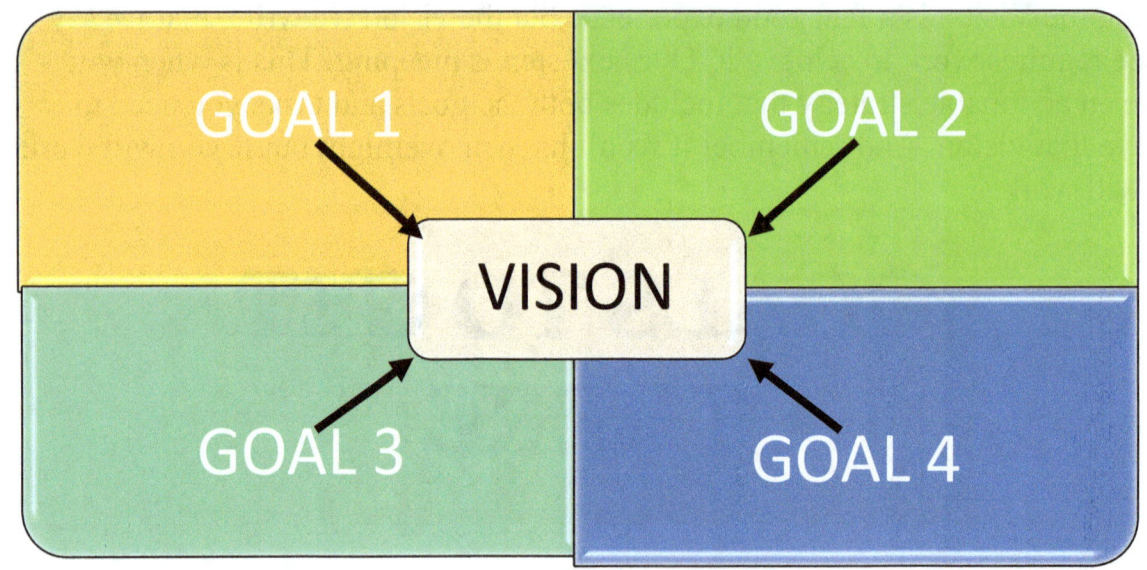

1. GOAL 1
Action Task:
Action Task:
Action Task:

2. GOAL 2
Action Task:
Action Task:
Action Task:

3. GOAL 3
Action Task:
Action Task:
Action Task:

4. GOAL 4
Action Task:
Action Task:
Action Task:

Turn Your Goals into Action oriented tasks by
- Assessing where you are and what actions you need to take to achieve your goals
- Document each step | Keyword & Emotion Along the way

In vision mapping, the vision should be as clear and as detailed as you can make it. The 5 W's apply here. The goals you set are your how!

1. Who is in the vision with you?
2. What is the vision?
3. When does the vision happen?
4. Where does the vision take place?
5. Why is this your vision?

Your Steps Are:
- Write the Vision
- Set the Goals to the vision.
- Break the goals up into daily tasks for you to work on
- Create Action Steps for each task to achieve the goals and fulfill the vision
- Write the vision in present tense. In a now conversation. This is key. The way you speak to your vision, its tasks, its goals will determine how hard you work towards it | How long you will take to achieve it and if God can trust you with it.

Write the vision and make *it* plain on tablets, that he may run who reads it. For the vision *is* yet for an appointed time; But at the end it will speak, and it will not lie. – Habakkuk 2:2-3

When is the appointed time?

The Discretionary Impartation

THE TIMING OF THE OCULAR & INTERNAL RELEASE

Timing is pivotal in the release of vision and it starts from the inside. The exoneration from what held you bound began when you were broken, when you came face to face with a reality that you have lived.

God does not operate in the time we do, by years, by months, by days, by hours, by minutes and by seconds. His calendar is created different.

Ecclesiastes 3:1 says: *To everything there is a season, and a time to every purpose under heaven*

In reading that scripture we understand that we live in a time that changes. We pass between 2 happenings, both identifiable by our emotions and our ability to see the purpose in them.

Paul's conversation took place on a road between his old life and his delivered life where lied the assignment God had for him. It was the season and the appointed time in Gods purpose and here's why.

Paul reminds us that he was a persecutor of the church who had a zealous devotion to Jewish traditions. He grew up in a strict household where the Old Testament was law, so he was well versed in biblical scripture. The two are intertwined by inclination. Hearing of a risen savior that some called Son of David, others called Messiah and more called Savior was a contraction to the tradition he had grown to believe, that had been embedded in his heart and mind in Judaism.

His ways were his life and in his mind he did not think any wrong of it. He said himself in:

Acts 22:3-4 I searched for Christians so that men could kill them. I arrested both men and women and threw them into prison.

Acts 22:20 Stephen died because he was a Christian. I was there when he died. I stood there. I approved of this. I guarded the clothes of those who killed him.

Acts 9:1, 2 Meanwhile, Saul was still planning to murder the disciples of Jesus. He went to the most important priest and asked him for letters to the rulers of the synagogues in Damascus. If he found any Christians there, whether men or women, he would take them to Jerusalem. There he would put them in prison.

Acts 26:10-11 And that is just what I did in Jerusalem. On the authority of the most important priest, I put many Christians in prison. When men killed them, I voted against the Christians. Often I went from one synagogue to another to punish them. I wanted them to speak against God. I was so eager that I even went to foreign cities to find them.

He assumed the assignment of violently forcing believers to turn their back on what we know as truth for Jewish traditions.

The revelation of the risen Savior that Paul received did not come by flesh and blood but direct from God. He could not see the truth in what was in front of him despite the miracles, the signs and the wonders. All he saw was what he believed. His optical could not connect to the unvarnished truth that surrounded him but on Damascus he became what he already was and that was blind.

Gods will for your life is not subject to approval by man it is preordained. Every encounter Paul has while Saul was one step closer to meeting Jesus on Damascus. Think about that – What you did the moment before you realized you were walking in disbelief of who you are and the moment before you picked up Brave Vision– God had a plan already in place. It was pre-orchestrated

Has God spoken to your heart? Or is He speaking to you now?

Do you remember the moment He did it? Write it down. It means something

Brave Vision

Your Time

"As I made my journey and drew near to Damascus, about noon a great light from heaven suddenly shone about me. And I fell to the ground and heard a voice saying to me, 'Saul, Saul, why do you persecute me?'" (Acts 22:6-7)

It was noon! All scriptures in all versions say that the light came from heaven at a specific time. The time is symbolic because every day at noon Jewish men recited prayers while standing on their feet and looking toward Jerusalem. It was part of their customary traditions.

1. Was Paul then Saul in standing position observing prayer? And the encounter brought him to his knees.

God will use what we believe is customary | What we believe is tradition in our old ways | in our blind state to set us up for an encounter

Paul may have thought that he was going to look for Christians to persecute armed with letters of "permission" by Jewish leaders but God flipped the switch and changed his story.

Listen, no man can influence you more than you can influence yourself. This workbook is a tool that God allowed you to encounter to start the conversation to get to where you need to go in the areas you desire shift in, in your life. But when you seek great change | when you see a vision experience – There is no one but God who can reveal the truth of your DNA and show you that you are a perfect match to the assignment you almost aborted, the assignment you had in wait, the assignment you didn't believe you were good enough for.

When Ecclesiastes calls for us to live our lives with God's purposes in mind that scripture stands even through difficult times. I, to am guilty of not believing God for the things He purposed for my life because of what was embedded in my heart. My norm was not Gods assignment; it was contrary to it.

I believed I should be afraid because I walked in fear. I believed that I was unworthy of a healthy relationship because the men I had been with didn't show me that I was valued and giving myself away said that I did not value myself. I believed that my life would be full of alcoholism, addictions and domestic violence because what I thought were happy moments happened in midst of those things.

I am not going to use this workbook to give you my full testimony but I will tell you that I understand where you are, where you have been and Glory be to God where you are going in every area of your life.

God will use everything from your past and present to fulfill the assignment for your future. It's your arsenal ……

When you begin to believe with your heart and mind that you are:

- More than a conqueror
- That you are destined for greater
- That you are more than a number
- More than a curse word or an item
- More than how you feel
- More than what you see
- More than what people call you
- More than your mistakes
- More than your background check
- More than a diagnosis
- More than a heartbreak
- More than your bank account
- More than your car
- More than where you live
- More than your title
- More than an accessory on someone's arm
- More than the hurt and pain you have experienced
- More than your addictions
- More than your failures
- More than your social media profile
- More than an update status
- More than a quick text
- More than what you perceive yourself to be

God will activate your vision when you believe through revelation of what He has shown you.

The Bible says you are:
- A Kings Kid
- A Joint Heir
- Called of A Royal Priesthood
- A Warrior

And when you realize that some things have to break in order for what's inside to come out you will prep yourself to catch what's inside during the outpour.

Once your heart is lined up with the word, with the truth, God will open your eyes to see and like so many others who went through what we now call testimonies to get to where they are – God has a reason, a season, an assignment for why he has opened your eyes. Is it to See or Is It to Build

BRAVE VISION

THE SEER & THE BUILDER

Brave
VISION

Brave Vision

I say this in love but honestly with a righteous indignation: It's sometimes hard to remember that God has redeemed us all but when we think about people in the bible like Saul or Rahab the prostitute who God set free to see differently during an experience, it makes our own stories a bit more bearable. Especially if we have been the subject of finger pointing, accusations, slander and shame.

I know people can be mean I experienced someone sharing parts of my testimony I had only shared in a private setting to others as a way to hinder a door from opening and this is what I learned. If God is for you who can be against you.

What I see, what you see is not determined by what someone says but by who God is. I have been name called, talked about, accused, shunned, embarrassed, taken advantage of, misinterpreted and straight cussed out to my face. Not by people I expected but by those who I kept close to me. People who had become comfortable with me waddling in my mess and misery. People who were upset to see the change in my life and were upset to see me run after a purpose that they did not understand or could comprehend because it was not for them. The Eye (I) Chart was custom created for Khalilah and yours was custom created for you.

Our ability to walk whole in completeness is contingent on our ability to believe. To activate our God senses and engage in the truth of his word, his power, his authority and in his grace. Now let me be clear there is a cost that comes with grace. In the book the cost of discipleship, it talks about grace not being a treasure chest that we can tap into whenever we need because we know that in John 1:9 God is just to forgive us of our sins but understand it is a place to find redemption because of the cross where we can admit our struggle and find the help we need to pursue the one that forgives.

After learning about yourself through the I chart | going back to your history and identifying the symptoms that led to the reactive emotions | Rejoicing in your divine appointment at your own personal Damascus refraction where you received the building tools you needed for the discretionary impartation, ask yourself; are you really ready to See? Are you ready to walk in Brave Vision – The ability to see with the I and not just the eyes because with it comes the charge to build. The accountability of accepting the call on our lives to be more than what we thought we were because it is our God ordained destiny. It is an assignment that was given to us by name. I went from Khalilah to Daughter of the King. I went from Khalilah to a Proverbs 31 woman. I went from Khalilah to joint heir in Christ and so have you.

A **Seer** is a person endowed with profound moral and spiritual insight or knowledge.

A **Builder** is a person who constructs something by putting parts or material together over a period of time.

I know you are wondering why can't I do both. Why is there an & in between the 2 words we just defined as if it is separate? Let me explain when Paul received his vision to see God, he did not immediately go to build- he went through the groundbreaking but did not have the blueprint for the assignment. The most important component of walking in Brave Vision is understanding Gods timing.

You have to go through a season of seeing, a season of breaking to get the blueprints for what God wants you to build. If you try to build first you may miss something because you don't have all the information you need.

It's similar to building a house, you just don't start the process before knowing what the foundation will be made up of, how many square feet it will be, how many rooms will be in it, what will the walls look like and what color paint should go inside.

Our lives and the lives we will impact are the same way. When you walk in who you are called to be let God give you the direction and don't try to do it alone. That's what caused our vision to be impaired in the first place. We stopped listening, stopped believing what He said and listened to what everyone else said or did and followed suit.

When you know that it is time to execute the vision that you wrote down in this workbook or another that you may have in your life. The pieces will begin to fall together if you can comprehend going from Chrono's' to Kairos'. From man's time to Gods time.

What I missed by being bound by fear for more than a decade, I am watching God expedite. I understood that my laying low, my bound moments, my brokenness was part of the process that led me back to believing what it is the bible says about me and when I glanced at my I chart I saw the oak tree in the acorn, the flower fully bloomed from the seed- it was then the release came and I stepped out on faith to Kingdom Build.

Brave Vision

Are you ready to do the same?

How do you I know it's the right time? Ask yourself these questions

Have you written down the vision and made it plain?
YES ( ) NO ( )

If you answered No Write it now. If you need a boost head back to the discretionary impartation

Have you prayed and asked God for forgiveness for what you've done & healing from what you experienced?
YES ( ) NO ( )

If you answered No write your prayer here and date it. If you need a boost head back to the Power of Prayer

Do you feel good about yourself?
YES ( ) NO ( )

If you answered No repeat these declarations and write down why ? If you need a boost head back to the I Am section

I Have Been Fearfully & Wonderfully Made. God is the source of my strength. I walk in redemption through Him to be my best version of who he called me to be. I am not my past, I am not my failures, I am who the bible says I am and I will do what the bible says I can do. My victory is tied to the cross. When Jesus Got up on the 3rd day – He got up for me so that I can rise from what I thought would take me out into the life he has for me. God has hand on

Brave Vision

me. He has always had his hands on me. From this day forth I will see me through the word and I will stand. I will walk in Godfidence. The confidence of Christ.

Now write down Why you don't feel good about yourself. Is it because of what someone else said or did? Is it because of something you did?

Did the declarations help? Did heading back to the I AM section inspire you? If you are still stuck go back and scan the QR CODE

Does the vision feel impossible?
YES ( )   NO ( )

If you answered yes, you are on track. It may feel impossible to us but it is possible in God. Write down what resources you need here from your mapping. Remember turn Big Vision into Goals and then actionable tasks. 1 step at a time is 1 step closer.

Finally, are you in a place where you are ready spiritually, professionally and emotionally to commit to the vision no matter what you face, no matter what you see because you believe God?
YES ( )   NO ( )

If you answered yes. Declare this right now: God I am ready | I am committed | Use me for your Glory. This Vision belongs to you and I am just a vessel so have your way, in me, through me and for me.

If you answered No, ask yourself what is holding you back. If you still need a boost head back to the Building tools so that you can dig deep, plant seeds and get rid of the trash so that you can move forward. If you still need help – Email me and let's talk at Khalilah@KhalilahOlokunola.com

Brave Vision

Historically, the bible and our own personal lives is filled with stories of people who have overcome difficult challenges and pressed forward to achieve great things and their dexterity to do so is no different than ours. We have to want it. Do you want it?

The most crucial moments of my life happened when I said yes to God. My yes was connected to someone else and when I became conscious of that, conscious that my tears could no longer be my excuse it gave me the strength to try and rise. God always met me at my place of intention with an even now experience.

When Lazarus was in the tomb Martha complained of what it would smell like if the rock was rolled away but the bible says that when the rock moved the Lord called Lazarus by name to come forth and he did, in grave clothes where the disciples were commanded to unwrap him. It was there the bible says that many who came to see what Jesus had done grew faith in him.

1st – Get rid of Martha, she will stop your blessing
2nd – Know that a delay doesn't mean denied. God may not always show up and manifest when you call but he always shows up on time.
3rd – When you hear the call it doesn't matter what state you are in, be obedient and come forth.
4th – God will surround you with people that will help you unwrap the bandages. Be prayerful, be discerning and make sure you identify those people. Be willing to accept their help.
5th – The many that grew faith in him did it because you came forth out of your dead place.

Your neighbors are waiting for you to come forth
Your spouse is waiting for you to come forth
Your kids are waiting for you to come forth
Your parents are waiting for you to come forth
Your co-workers are waiting for you to come forth
Your classmates are waiting for you to come forth
Those that hurt you are even waiting for you to come forth

The faith of some people is directly connected to your YES – (SHOUT NOW). We never know who God wants to bring out with our Yes! Who he wants to deliver and set free.

You Have to see It, to build It

Brave Vision

When people see you overcome the challenges that you have faced in boldness, in faith and in God, they are going to want to know how you did it and you need to tell them "But God", I can see me!

Do you understand what I just said – It doesn't matter where you are or where you have been. God created you, he purposed you and he assigned you! Brave Vision is not a cliché' or a catchy title to get your attention it is the manifestation I experienced walking despite being fearful of what people would say or do because of the past hurt and shortcomings that became a part of my story.

That day when I had to choose between hitting the boy who was my friend or my mother spanking me, I chose to hit him instead and all the kids on the block rejected me. That rejection caused hurt , pain and rebellion that came with reactive emotions. Emotions that caused more catastrophes in my life . Like anyone else , I did desire a glimpse of the glory. I wanted Brave Vision. And I want to be able to tell you that I had achieved it but when I made it to Damascus, got all the way to straight street, *The scales finally fell from my eyes – I could actually see some of me and I loved what I saw but in a moments time I had circled around and found myself back on the same road again. I understood where I was and where I was headed. The sustained blindness and reactive emotions disassociated my heart with my reality and caused me to lose the only thing I had left…. my name - but that's another story.* ~

BRAVE VISION
21 DAY PLANNER
MAKE VISION A HABIT

MONTHLY FOCUS

- ☐ ....
- ☐ ....
- ☐ ....
- ☐ ....
- ☐ ....

DATES TO REMEMBER

....
....
....
....
....
....
....

I SEE ME NOTES

GOALS

- ☐ ....
- ☐ ....
- ☐ ....
- ☐ ....
- ☐ ....
- ☐ ....
- ☐ ....
- ☐ ....
- ☐ ....
- ☐ ....

You Have to see It, to build It

BRAVE VISION
21 DAY PLANNER
MAKE VISION A HABIT

MONTHLY FOCUS

- [ ] ....
- [ ] ....
- [ ] ....
- [ ] ....
- [ ] ....

DATES TO REMEMBER

....
....
....
....
....

I SEE ME NOTES

GOALS

- [ ] ....
- [ ] ....
- [ ] ....
- [ ] ....
- [ ] ....
- [ ] ....
- [ ] ....
- [ ] ....
- [ ] ....
- [ ] ....
- [ ] ....

BRAVE VISION
21 DAY PLANNER
MAKE VISION A HABIT

MONTHLY FOCUS

- [ ] ....
- [ ] ....
- [ ] ....
- [ ] ....
- [ ] ....

DATES TO REMEMBER

....
....
....
....
....

I SEE ME NOTES

GOALS

- [ ] ....
- [ ] ....
- [ ] ....
- [ ] ....
- [ ] ....
- [ ] ....
- [ ] ....
- [ ] ....
- [ ] ....
- [ ] ....
- [ ] ....
- [ ] ....

BRAVE VISION
21 DAY PLANNER
MAKE VISION A HABIT

MONTHLY FOCUS

☐ ....
☐ ....
☐ ....
☐ ....
☐ ....

DATES TO REMEMBER

....
....
....
....
....

I SEE ME NOTES

GOALS

☐ ....
☐ ....
☐ ....
☐ ....
☐ ....
☐ ....
☐ ....
☐ ....
☐ ....
☐ ....
☐ ....

BRAVE VISION
21 DAY PLANNER
MAKE VISION A HABIT

MONTHLY FOCUS

- ☐ ....
- ☐ ....
- ☐ ....
- ☐ ....
- ☐ ....

DATES TO REMEMBER

....
....
....
....
....

I SEE ME NOTES

GOALS

- ☐ ....
- ☐ ....
- ☐ ....
- ☐ ....
- ☐ ....
- ☐ ....
- ☐ ....
- ☐ ....
- ☐ ....
- ☐ ....
- ☐ ....

BRAVE VISION
21 DAY PLANNER
MAKE VISION A HABIT

MONTHLY FOCUS

☐ ....
☐ ....
☐ ....
☐ ....
☐ ....

DATES TO REMEMBER

....
....
....
....
....

I SEE ME NOTES

GOALS

☐ ....
☐ ....
☐ ....
☐ ....
☐ ....
☐ ....
☐ ....
☐ ....
☐ ....
☐ ....
☐ ....

BRAVE VISION
21 DAY PLANNER
MAKE VISION A HABIT

MONTHLY FOCUS

- ☐ ....
- ☐ ....
- ☐ ....
- ☐ ....
- ☐ ....

DATES TO REMEMBER

....
....
....
....
....
....

I SEE ME NOTES

GOALS

- ☐ ....
- ☐ ....
- ☐ ....
- ☐ ....
- ☐ ....
- ☐ ....
- ☐ ....
- ☐ ....
- ☐ ....
- ☐ ....
- ☐ ....
- ☐ ....

BRAVE VISION
21 DAY PLANNER
MAKE VISION A HABIT

MONTHLY FOCUS

- ☐ ....
- ☐ ....
- ☐ ....
- ☐ ....
- ☐ ....

DATES TO REMEMBER

....
....
....
....
....

I SEE ME NOTES

GOALS

- ☐ ....
- ☐ ....
- ☐ ....
- ☐ ....
- ☐ ....
- ☐ ....
- ☐ ....
- ☐ ....
- ☐ ....
- ☐ ....
- ☐ ....

BRAVE VISION
21 DAY PLANNER
MAKE VISION A HABIT

MONTHLY FOCUS

- ☐ ....
- ☐ ....
- ☐ ....
- ☐ ....
- ☐ ....

DATES TO REMEMBER

....
....
....
....
....

I SEE ME NOTES

GOALS

- ☐ ....
- ☐ ....
- ☐ ....
- ☐ ....
- ☐ ....
- ☐ ....
- ☐ ....
- ☐ ....
- ☐ ....
- ☐ ....
- ☐ ....

BRAVE VISION
21 DAY PLANNER
MAKE VISION A HABIT

MONTHLY FOCUS

- ☐ ....
- ☐ ....
- ☐ ....
- ☐ ....
- ☐ ....

DATES TO REMEMBER

....
....
....
....
....

I SEE ME NOTES

GOALS

- ☐ ....
- ☐ ....
- ☐ ....
- ☐ ....
- ☐ ....
- ☐ ....
- ☐ ....
- ☐ ....
- ☐ ....
- ☐ ....
- ☐ ....

BRAVE VISION
21 DAY PLANNER
MAKE VISION A HABIT

MONTHLY FOCUS

- ☐ ....
- ☐ ....
- ☐ ....
- ☐ ....
- ☐ ....

DATES TO REMEMBER

....
....
....
....
....

I SEE ME NOTES

GOALS

- ☐ ....
- ☐ ....
- ☐ ....
- ☐ ....
- ☐ ....
- ☐ ....
- ☐ ....
- ☐ ....
- ☐ ....
- ☐ ....
- ☐ ....

BRAVE VISION
21 DAY PLANNER
MAKE VISION A HABIT

MONTHLY FOCUS

☐ ....
☐ ....
☐ ....
☐ ....
☐ ....

DATES TO REMEMBER

....
....
....
....
....

I SEE ME NOTES

GOALS

☐ ....
☐ ....
☐ ....
☐ ....
☐ ....
☐ ....
☐ ....
☐ ....
☐ ....
☐ ....
☐ ....

BRAVE VISION
21 DAY PLANNER
MAKE VISION A HABIT

MONTHLY FOCUS

- ☐ ....
- ☐ ....
- ☐ ....
- ☐ ....
- ☐ ....

DATES TO REMEMBER

....
....
....
....
....
....
....

I SEE ME NOTES

GOALS

- ☐ ....
- ☐ ....
- ☐ ....
- ☐ ....
- ☐ ....
- ☐ ....
- ☐ ....
- ☐ ....
- ☐ ....
- ☐ ....
- ☐ ....

You Have to see It, to build It

BRAVE VISION
21 DAY PLANNER
MAKE VISION A HABIT

MONTHLY FOCUS

- ☐ ....
- ☐ ....
- ☐ ....
- ☐ ....
- ☐ ....

DATES TO REMEMBER

....
....
....
....
....

I SEE ME NOTES

GOALS

- ☐ ....
- ☐ ....
- ☐ ....
- ☐ ....
- ☐ ....
- ☐ ....
- ☐ ....
- ☐ ....
- ☐ ....
- ☐ ....
- ☐ ....

BRAVE VISION
21 DAY PLANNER
MAKE VISION A HABIT

MONTHLY FOCUS

- ☐ ....
- ☐ ....
- ☐ ....
- ☐ ....
- ☐ ....

DATES TO REMEMBER

....
....
....
....
....

I SEE ME NOTES

GOALS

- ☐ ....
- ☐ ....
- ☐ ....
- ☐ ....
- ☐ ....
- ☐ ....
- ☐ ....
- ☐ ....
- ☐ ....
- ☐ ....

BRAVE VISION
21 DAY PLANNER
MAKE VISION A HABIT

MONTHLY FOCUS

- ☐ ....
- ☐ ....
- ☐ ....
- ☐ ....
- ☐ ....

DATES TO REMEMBER

....
....
....
....
....

I SEE ME NOTES

GOALS

- ☐ ....
- ☐ ....
- ☐ ....
- ☐ ....
- ☐ ....
- ☐ ....
- ☐ ....
- ☐ ....
- ☐ ....
- ☐ ....
- ☐ ....

BRAVE VISION
21 DAY PLANNER
MAKE VISION A HABIT

MONTHLY FOCUS

☐ ....
☐ ....
☐ ....
☐ ....
☐ ....

DATES TO REMEMBER

....
....
....
....
....
....

I SEE ME NOTES

GOALS

☐ ....
☐ ....
☐ ....
☐ ....
☐ ....
☐ ....
☐ ....
☐ ....
☐ ....
☐ ....

You Have to see It, to build It

BRAVE VISION
21 DAY PLANNER
MAKE VISION A HABIT

MONTHLY FOCUS

- [ ] ....
- [ ] ....
- [ ] ....
- [ ] ....
- [ ] ....

DATES TO REMEMBER

....
....
....
....
....

I SEE ME NOTES

GOALS

- [ ] ....
- [ ] ....
- [ ] ....
- [ ] ....
- [ ] ....
- [ ] ....
- [ ] ....
- [ ] ....
- [ ] ....
- [ ] ....
- [ ] ....

BRAVE VISION
21 DAY PLANNER
MAKE VISION A HABIT

MONTHLY FOCUS

- ☐ ....
- ☐ ....
- ☐ ....
- ☐ ....
- ☐ ....

DATES TO REMEMBER

....
....
....
....
....

I SEE ME NOTES

GOALS

- ☐ ....
- ☐ ....
- ☐ ....
- ☐ ....
- ☐ ....
- ☐ ....
- ☐ ....
- ☐ ....
- ☐ ....
- ☐ ....
- ☐ ....

You Have to see It, to build It

BRAVE VISION
21 DAY PLANNER
MAKE VISION A HABIT

MONTHLY FOCUS

- [ ] ....
- [ ] ....
- [ ] ....
- [ ] ....
- [ ] ....

DATES TO REMEMBER

....

....

....

....

....

I SEE ME NOTES

GOALS

- [ ] ....
- [ ] ....
- [ ] ....
- [ ] ....
- [ ] ....
- [ ] ....
- [ ] ....
- [ ] ....
- [ ] ....
- [ ] ....
- [ ] ....

BRAVE VISION
21 DAY PLANNER
MAKE VISION A HABIT

MONTHLY FOCUS

- ☐ ....
- ☐ ....
- ☐ ....
- ☐ ....
- ☐ ....

DATES TO REMEMBER

....
....
....
....
....

I SEE ME NOTES

GOALS

- ☐ ....
- ☐ ....
- ☐ ....
- ☐ ....
- ☐ ....
- ☐ ....
- ☐ ....
- ☐ ....
- ☐ ....
- ☐ ....
- ☐ ....

You Have to see It, to build It

BRAVE VISION
21 DAY PLANNER
MAKE VISION A HABIT

MONTHLY FOCUS

- ☐ ....
- ☐ ....
- ☐ ....
- ☐ ....
- ☐ ....

DATES TO REMEMBER

....
....
....
....
....

I SEE ME NOTES

GOALS

- ☐ ....
- ☐ ....
- ☐ ....
- ☐ ....
- ☐ ....
- ☐ ....
- ☐ ....
- ☐ ....
- ☐ ....
- ☐ ....

I See Me Differently

-NOTES-

BRAVE VISION

I See Me Differently

-NOTES-

BRAVE VISION

I See Me Differently

-NOTES-

BRAVE VISION

I See Me Differently

-NOTES-

BRAVE VISION

I See Me Differently

-NOTES-

BRAVE VISION

I See Me Differently

-NOTES-

BRAVE VISION

I See Me Differently

-NOTES-

BRAVE VISION

I See Me Differently

-NOTES-

I See Me Differently

-NOTES-

BRAVE VISION

I See Me Differently

-NOTES-

BRAVE VISION

I See Me Differently

-NOTES-

BRAVE VISION

I See Me Differently

-NOTES-

www.ingramcontent.com/pod-product-compliance
Lightning Source LLC
Chambersburg PA
CBHW060529010526
44110CB00052B/2540